KU-275-224

VHF radio
including GMDSS

© RYA 2008
2nd Edition

The Royal Yachting Association
RYA House, Ensign Way
Hamble, Southampton
Hampshire SO31 4YA

Tel: 0845 345 0400
Fax: 0845 345 0329
E-mail: publications@rya.org.uk
Web: www.rya.org.uk

ISBN 9781906435202
RYA Order Code G22

Published by **The Royal Yachting Association**
RYA House Ensign Way Hamble Southampton SO31 4YA
Tel: +44 (0)845 345 0400
Fax: +44 (0)845 345 0329
Email: publications@rya.org.uk
Web: www.rya.org.uk
© 2008 Royal Yachting Association
All rights reserved.

Note: While all reasonable care has been taken in the
preparation of this book, the publisher takes no
responsibility for the use of the methods or products or
contracts described in the book.

Cover design & typesetting: Batt Creative

Edited by: Alison Noice

Proof-reading: Alan Thatcher

Printed in China through World Print

CONTENTS

INTRODUCTION

Marine communications have been revolutionised by the introduction of the Global Maritime Distress and Safety System (GMDSS). Designed by the International Maritime Organisation and supported by the International Telecommunication Union, it ensures that ships anywhere in the world can communicate with an onshore Rescue Co-ordination Centre by two independent means without the need for a specialist radio operator.

Yachts and Small Craft are not bound to carry radio transmitters and receivers and are under no obligation to participate in the GMDSS. However, any yachtsman who wants to communicate with other ships, harbour authorities and Rescue Co-ordination Centres, needs to keep reasonably up-to-date with the equipment and techniques of the commercial shipping world.

Some elements of pre-GMDSS communication will continue to be available but it will become increasingly important for the yachtsman to participate in the GMDSS if they want to be certain of the ability to send a quick, effective distress message.

Although in inshore waters mobile phones have proven to be effective, they are not a substitute for a marine VHF radio. They do not have the ability to participate in an open network or receive and transmit broadcast messages such as urgency and safety messages. They can prove useful in emergencies when there is no marine VHF radio on board.

The continuing strength of maritime VHF is the facility to provide both discrete ship to ship or shore station conversations and broadcast messages.

With hundreds of thousands of users sharing just 59 international channels there have to be rules and procedures which are understood and followed by everyone. They don't have to be followed slavishly but if they are totally ignored, communication would be impossible.

The purpose of this book is to explain how boaters can join the international community of VHF marine radiotelephony, providing for their own safety without interfering with other users.

LICENSING

THE REQUIREMENT

When fitting a VHF radiotelephone, the owner of any vessel must make sure that they satisfy three requirements:

1. The equipment being fitted must be "type approved".
2. The equipment must be licensed.
3. The operator must be licensed or be under the direct supervision of someone who holds an operator's licence.

Type approval

Marine radio equipment offered for sale in the UK must conform to the technical requirements of the European Radio and Telecommunications Terminal Equipment Directive (R&TTE) and should carry an identification mark similar to the one shown in fig 1.1. In addition, the equipment or the handbook accompanying it should have a Declaration of Conformity stating that it meets the needs of the R&TTE Directive, which ensures that sets operate in a range of conditions and do not cause interference with other users.

Fig 1.1

Second hand sets or those bought overseas may not be fitted with the correct channels and often do not conform to the European standard, and could be confiscated if found onboard if Office of Communications (Ofcom) staff carry out one of their routine inspections.

The Ofcom website has information on all the radio regulations so if you have any doubts about your own equipment consult Ofcom on www.ofcom.org.uk or telephone them on 0845 456 300.

The RYA (Royal Yachting Association) and the Maritime & Coastguard Agency (MCA) are always willing to assist with questions on procedure and may be contacted as follows:

RYA at www.rya.org.uk and MCA on 023 8032 9100.

The Ship Radio Licence

The Wireless Telegraphy Act of 1949 requires that all vessels fitted with radio equipment have a valid Ship Radio Licence. This licence is valid for the lifetime of the vessel but owners are required to renew it every ten years or if equipment is changed. It is free of charge if the initial application and renewal is completed on line using the Ofcom website, but postal applications carry a charge of £20.00.

When first applying for a licence the applicant will be invited to open a "user account" and will be sent a password for any future communications. Ofcom will advise the owner about renewal after ten years.

It is important that the licence is carried on board the boat especially when taking the boat out of UK waters where the inspection procedures are often more rigorous than those in the UK.

The ship's licence covers all items that transmit provided that they have been declared on the application form. It covers any or all of the following:

a) MF, HF or VHF radiotelephone equipment.

b) Digital selective calling (DSC) equipment associated with the GMDSS.

c) Hand held marine VHF radios used on the parent craft or in the tender.

d) Radar and Search and Rescue Transponders (SARTs).

e) Emergency Positioning Radio Beacons (EPIRBs) using 406MHz, 121.5/ 243MHz or 1.6 GHz.

f) Satellite communications equipment (Ship Earth Stations).

g) Low power on board communications including UHF and repeater stations.

Upon the original application, boats will be issued with a unique international call sign, which remains with the vessel through both change of ownership and equipment. DSC equipment will also be issued with a nine-figure identifying number called a Maritime Mobile Service Identity or MMSI for short. MMSIs are discussed on Page 13.

Ship Portable Licence

A handheld VHF radio which is intended for use in a variety of craft is required to have a "Ship Portable Licence", which is free online and £20.00 by post. This set will be issued with an international call sign which includes the letter "T" to denote that it is "transportable" and licensed to an individual and not a vessel. A typical call sign would be MZD8T.

Licences for radios used by Yacht Clubs

In the UK licences are available, which permit yacht clubs and similar organisations to establish a base station. Full details are given in the Coastal Station Radio information booklet available from the Ofcom website (ofcom.org.uk) or from:

Ofcom, Riverside House, 2a Southwark Bridge Road, London SE1 9HA.

Telephone: 0207 981 3000.

Operator Qualifications

To maintain operational standards and ensure a working knowledge of distress, emergency and safety procedures, a maritime radio can only be operated by a holder of the appropriate operator's licence or by someone under their direct personal supervision.

The MCA have contracted the RYA to conduct examinations and issue licences for the Marine VHF Short Range Certificate (SRC). For anyone venturing much further offshore, the AMERC Organisation runs a similar scheme for the Long Range Certificate. (See www.amerc.ac.uk).

The MCA are responsible to the European Telecommunications Union (CEPT) for operator standards within the United Kingdom and Northern Ireland. CEPT member states will accept the validity of UK certificates for use on British registered craft but it would be wise to ask advice from the MCA when operating in foreign-flagged vessels.

Most candidates for the SRC are taught and assessed during an 8-hour course at a RYA Training Centre. Those who pass are granted the licence, which has two parts:

Part 1 - Certificate of Competence, which is awarded for having the knowledge required to operate a marine VHF set effectively.

Part 2 - Authority to Operate, which gives holders of Part 1, aged 16 and above, governmental permission to operate a VHF radio on a British ship.

Young persons under the age of 16 are actively encouraged to attend an SRC course and will be awarded the Certificate of Competence on successful completion of the course. However, the Authority to Operate will be post-dated to their 16th birthday.

Holders of non-DSC VHF Operator's Certificates

Holders of the Restricted Certificate of Competence (VHF) only, which was issued prior to the introduction of the SRC may continue to operate non-DSC radios but must have knowledge of the Global Maritime Distress and Safety Scheme. If they intend to operate DSC equipment, they must qualify for the SRC at an RYA Training Centre either by attending a course or by direct examination.

RYA Training Centres

A list of RYA Training Centres running SRC Courses is available from the RYA, Tel: 0845 345 0384, email: training@rya.org.uk or from the RYA website: www.ryatraining.org.uk. Full details of the syllabus and example examination questions are contained in the RYA booklet G26.

MANAGEMENT OF THE MARITIME MOBILE BAND

THE VHF INTERNATIONAL MARITIME MOBILE BAND

VHF frequencies between 156.00MHz and 174.00MHz are allocated to the Maritime Mobile Service (MMS); for use by ships fitted with VHF radio. This allocation is made by international agreement to maintain order into what would otherwise be a chaotic situation.

The band is divided into 59 channels with spacing of 25kHz between each (as listed in Annex C). In addition, national authorities allocate a number of private channels.

Simplex and duplex working

With simplex, (found in virtually all leisure craft and small workboats), transmission is only possible in one direction at a time; you can either transmit or receive but not both simultaneously. The single antenna is switched from receive to transmit (and back again) by using the press-to-transmit switch.

Duplex transmissions make it possible to transmit and receive simultaneously. It needs two frequencies and usually two antennas or a special duplex filter.

Ship-to-shore working channels are allocated on a two-frequency basis; for example, Ch26 has two frequencies - the ship transmits on a frequency of 157.3MHz and the shore station transmits on 161.9MHz.

It is possible to use simplex equipment on the two frequency channels, but transmission is still only possible in one direction at a time. The press-to-transmit switch automatically selects the correct frequency for transmission or reception.

Semi-duplex systems have simplex at one end and duplex at the other and two frequencies are required. It is virtually the same as simplex working but saves the duplex operator having to release the press-to-transmit switch during the conversation.

It's important to note that two ships are incapable of holding a conversation on duplex frequencies and therefore all inter-ship channels are simplex.

International channels

Each channel is allocated for one or more of eight specific purposes and it is important to select a suitable channel for your particular use:

• Distress safety and calling

Channel 16 - has always been the VHF Distress Safety and Calling frequency and will remain so for the foreseeable future. The normal routine is to establish contact on Ch16 and arrange to move to a mutually acceptable working frequency as quickly as possible. However, with the number of radio telephones in use, in the busiest areas, there is great pressure on Ch16 and rescue centres fear that a distress call may be missed due to congestion. Although all ships are encouraged to maintain a continuous watch on Ch16 when at sea, callers are encouraged to use working frequencies for initial calls whenever possible; this can only be done if the station called is maintaining a listening watch on that frequency.

The introduction of DSC, discussed in more on page 13, reduces congestion on Ch16 as the initial electronic alert is sent as a very short data burst using Ch70.

Ch70 must never be used for voice communication.

• Bridge-to-bridge

Channel 13 - is an inter-ship channel reserved exclusively for bridge-to-bridge communication on matters of navigational safety.

• Inter-ship

Channels 6, 8, 72 and 77 - should be used for inter-ship working because they are exclusively for that purpose. Other inter-ship channels are allocated for additional purposes; for example Ch10 for pollution control and Ch9 for harbour pilots (see Annex C). Small Craft should avoid using these channels.

• Port operations

Channels 11, 12 and 14 - most commonly used for port operations but refer to a nautical almanac for local variations.

• Ship movements (very similar to port operations)

Ship movements are often conducted on the single frequency channels such as **Ch15, 17 and 69**

• UK Small Craft Safety

Channel 67 - is single frequency ship-to-ship and is used by HM Coastguard (HMCG) as the Small Ship Safety Channel (UK only).

• Public correspondence

Channels allocated for public correspondence use two frequencies and are seldom used for link calls to shore. HM Coastguard is using some of them for weather forecasts and navigational warnings.

Private channels

A number of private channels, simplex and duplex, are allocated for national use. **ChD** is used by the MCA, to control distress and safety traffic. Others are allocated to organisations such as ferry companies and harbour tug operators for internal use. Sailing Schools may apply for a private channel and a fee is payable. Certain frequencies outside the International Maritime Band can also be allocated for private use.

With the exception of ChM and M2 a normal Ship Radio Licence does not include the use of any of these private channels and unmodified radios fitted in Small Craft cannot receive them.

National variations

The International Telecommunications Union (ITU) permits national authorities to modify the international frequency allocation to suit local operating procedures, the main UK variations are:

Channel M - a private simplex channel on 157.85MHz, one of two available to British yacht clubs for safety boats and race control, shown on some VHF sets as **P1 or 37**. A normal Ship Licence permits all craft to use this frequency, **but only in UK waters.**

Since yacht clubs are not fitted with Ch16 the initial call must be made on ChM if that is the listed working frequency.

Channel M2 - the other frequency available for use by British yacht clubs. It uses a simplex frequency of 161.425MHz and is included in UK Ship Licences, now the preferred channel for yacht race management but may not be available on some older VHF equipment.

Channel 80 - duplex channel for use by UK marinas and ships calling them. Since marinas are not fitted with Ch16 the initial call must be made on Ch80 if that is the listed frequency. Marinas are restricted to transmitting on 1 watt only, so a vessel calling a marina from a distance on 25w is unlikely to hear the reply from the marina.

GMDSS

WHAT IS THE GMDSS?

Early in the twentieth century, it became possible to send messages by radio and ships began to use the Morse Code for distress messages and routine communications. Radio operators were trained to listen for other vessels in distress which significantly reduced shipping losses and loss of life.

By the 1970s, ships had increased in size and advances in radio technology meant that voice communication was possible. Morse Code operators became redundant and reliance was placed on watch keeping officers listening for distressed vessels.

Shipping losses continued to worry the International Maritime Organisation (IMO) and to address this they introduced the Global Maritime Distress and Safety System.

The system requires that ships be fitted with equipment which ensures that a casualty can alert Search and Rescue organisations and other ships. Pressing a single red button can send a digital distress alert, which gives both the identity and the position of the casualty - the whole process taking just a few seconds.

GMDSS regulations are compulsory for all commercial vessels over 300 gross register tons, fishing vessels and craft carrying 13 or more passengers in open water areas. These vessels are referred to as "compulsory fit" vessels, who have to carry the following equipment:

VHF DSC marine radio (and MF/HF if in areas other than A1)

406 MHz Emergency Position Indicating Radio Beacon

Search and Rescue Radar Transponder

Radar

Navtex

Waterproof hand held VHF

Smaller vessels are not covered by these rules and are referred to as "voluntary fit" but are strongly advised to fit DSC (Digital Selective Calling) sets so that they can also summon help quickly and efficiently. Although "compulsory fit" ships have been asked to continue to monitor the distress and calling frequency, Channel 16, for the foreseeable future greater reliance is placed on hearing an audible alert rather than a voice message. HM Coastguard, responsible for the integrity of Channel 16 in the UK, will continue to monitor the channel in the future but are very keen that leisure craft fit VHF DSC.

GMDSS areas

The world has been divided into four GMDSS areas and the radio equipment that vessels must carry depends on the sea areas in which they sail. The areas in NW Europe are shown in *Fig 3.1* below.

• Sea area A1

Within range of shore-based VHF Coast Stations fitted with DSC (30 to 50 miles, depending upon height of aerial).

• Sea area A2

Within range of shore-based MF/HF Coast Stations fitted with DSC (100 to 300 miles).

• Sea area A3

Within the coverage area of INMARSAT satellites (between 70°N and 70°S).

• Sea area A4

The remaining sea areas using HF DSC.

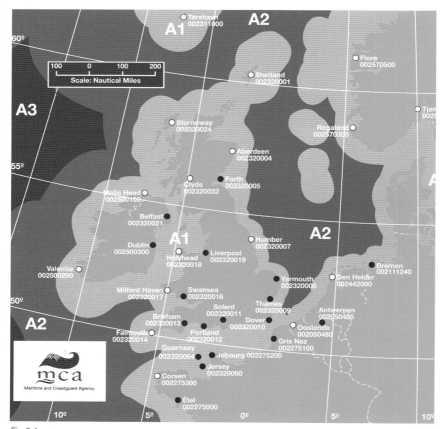

Fig 3.1

MARINE VHF & DIGITAL SELECTIVE CALLING EQUIPMENT

FITTING VHF

Position

The radiotelephone is usually located in the cabin of a small boat. It should be:

- securely fastened
- in a convenient position clear of spray and dampness
- away from the engine and any heat source

The set is connected to the yacht's power supply (observing the correct polarity) with the antenna feeder cable connected. No earth is needed. A waterproof extension loudspeaker, sited close to the steering position allows the helmsman to monitor the radio without disturbing crew who may be sleeping.

Power Supplies

While receiving, the radio consumes very little current. While transmitting, the current may rise to five or more amps. Generally, transmissions are infrequent and unlikely to present a serious drain on the boat's battery. However, some thought should be given, should the situation arise, when you need to send a distress message if the vessel is sinking and the main battery flooded. Under these circumstances a hand-held VHF radio with its own internal battery is essential.

Antennas

- The High Gain Antenna is about two metres long and concentrates the radiated power along a narrow horizontal beam giving greater ranges if the antenna is kept nearly vertical, as on a motor cruiser.
- The Unity Gain Antenna, about one metre long, has a radiated beam with a wider spread and, as it's less likely to be affected by heeling, is recommended for sailing yachts.

Ideally, the full power available from the transmitter should be radiated from the antenna but there will always be some loss in the feeder cable. Use the best quality available low loss cable from the radiotelephone to the antenna and keep the number of connectors or joins to a minimum.

The propagation of VHF radio waves is little more than line-of-sight so antenna height is very important. It's normally positioned at the masthead, any lower down it may be masked by the rigging, making communication difficult on certain relative bearings. A secondary, portable hand-held antenna will be invaluable on the day the rig is lost in a gale.

Care should be taken to avoid running the antenna feeder cable near other cables feeding sensitive equipment such as wind instruments, logs and electronic self steering equipment - even low loss cable will radiate.

Radio waves can be affected by various factors. High barometric pressure or increased humidity often give greater ranges than normal. Rough seas, causing the ship's antenna to sway back and forth will cause 'fluttering' and reduce the range considerably.

VHF EQUIPMENT

Features on VHF radios

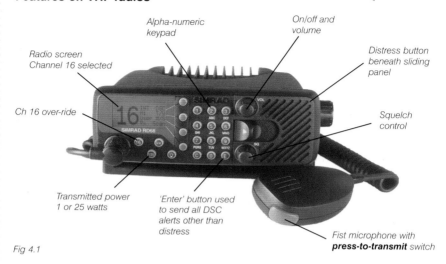

Alpha-numeric keypad

On/off and volume

Radio screen Channel 16 selected

Distress button beneath sliding panel

Ch 16 over-ride

Squelch control

Transmitted power 1 or 25 watts

'Enter' button used to send all DSC alerts other than distress

Fist microphone with **press-to-transmit** switch

Fig 4.1

On/off control and volume

The set in fig 4.1 has a combined on/off and volume control.

Squelch control

Reception is often accompanied by a background hiss; adjusting the squelch control will reduce the noise to acceptable levels. Be careful not to turn it up too much or distant and faint transmissions will be lost.

Press to transmit switch

When the press-to-transmit switch is depressed you can speak but not listen. Release it after speaking to hear the reply. This system of transmitting and receiving, called simplex, is explained on page 7.

Power output

The maximum permitted power output for small craft VHF in the Maritime Band is 25 watts but sets also have a low power output of about 1 watt. Whenever possible, this should be used as it transmits over a much shorter range and is less likely to interfere with other communications on the same frequency. When sets are first switched on 25 watts is automatically selected on many sets. Except in an emergency you should change to 1 watt before transmitting.

Distress button

The red distress button is found on sets fitted with Digital Selective Calling (DSC). It is activated only when the vessel to which it is fitted is in distress and is always protected in some way so that it cannot be activated by accident. If pressed once and then pressed again an audible signal will be heard as it progresses through a five second countdown sequence.

If it detects a DSC Distress alert, your VHF radio immediately tunes to Ch16 and sounds a loud buzzer. DSC is explained in more detail later in this chapter.

Channel 16 over-ride

Allows Ch16 (the International Distress, Safety and Calling frequency) to be selected without using the alpha-numeric key pad.

Dual watch (often labelled D/W)

Dual watch enables an operator to monitor Ch16 and one other selected channel. The receiver is switched to the selected channel but, when a transmission is detected on Ch16, it automatically switches over, reverting to the selected channel when the transmission ends. This means you can listen to, say, a port operations frequency while monitoring Ch16. Many sets offer triple watch where Ch16 and two other channels can be monitored.

Scanning

Any number of channels can be selected and the receiver listens to each in turn. If it receives a signal it remains on that channel until the transmission ends but if no incoming signal is received in a couple of seconds, it moves to the next selected channel. There is no priority for Ch16 so you cannot be certain that you have not missed an important transmission, particularly if a large number of channels is selected.

DIGITAL SELECTIVE CALLING (DSC)

The addition of DSC equipment to a marine VHF radio completely changes the method of making initial contact with other stations. This book covers Class D, the one usually found in Small Craft venturing up to 60 miles from a safe haven. All receivers in this class will be similar.

If GPS is interfaced with the DSC Controller, the position of a ship in distress will be included as part of the distress alert, giving sufficient information for a search to start. If GPS is not available, the ship's position should be entered manually at least every hour. If the position is more than 24 hours old, no position will be included in the distress alert.

General features

The DSC Controller is linked to, or is an integral part of, a conventional VHF radio. *Fig 4.1* shows an integrated set; the DSC component of two part equipment is illustrated later in the chapter. Just like a radio pager, the DSC Controller/Radio alerts another radio that it is being called and tells us that we must go to the radio to contact the caller. Thereafter the system is used like a conventional VHF radio.

A Distress Alert and an All-Ships call can always be sent, but to make a call to a specific ship or shore radio using your DSC Controller you must first know two things:

1. That the station to be called is fitted with DSC.
2. Its Maritime Mobile Service Identity (MMSI).

Maritime Mobile Service Identity (MMSI)

An MMSI is a unique nine digit number that identifies a particular ship or shore station. Those for ship stations are issued free of charge by the licensing authority and entered into the set on purchase. Each MMSI contains the country code, UK vessels being identified with the numbers 232, 233, 234 or 235.

Coast stations concerned with rescue coordination are identified with an MMSI beginning with two zeros. For example: Humber Coastguard's MMSI is 002320007. Important MMSIs are often listed in nautical almanacs and a searchable list of ship stations is kept by the ITU on their website: www.itu.int/MARS/.

If the vessel you wish to call is not listed you will need to obtain the MMSI from the boat owner.

There are four types of MMSI:

  a) Ship station
  b) Coast station (usually a Maritime Rescue Centre)
  c) Group station (programmable by the user, number allocated by Ofcom)
  d) Portable DSC equipment

13

All MMSIs contain nine digits but group and coast station numbers start with either one or two zeros to distinguish them from ship stations. Hand held VHF/DSC sets are allocated with an MMSI which begins with the digits 2359. For example:

M/V Abbotsgrange	UK Ship Station	232003556
Solent Coastguard	UK Coast Station	002320011
Nonsuch Yacht Charters	UK Group	023207823
Crosma Joburg	French Coast Station	002275200
M/V Bagot	Dutch Ship Station	244005297
Ten Islands Race	Eire Group	025000927
————	UK Portable DSC	235900498

DSC features

The Menu System

To use the DSC for anything other than a distress call it is necessary to understand the menu system, the information interface and guide to which will be found on the screen. Different manufacturers produce different layouts but they all provide similar functions which must conform to the specification for a Class D DSC Controller. *Fig 4.2* shows a typical menu.

HOME SCREEN	Call Log Menu
Call ▶▶	
ROUTINE DIRECTORY CALL	MMSI Channel ENTER
Any Numeric	
ROUTINE DIALLED CALL	Name Channel ENTER
▶▶	
SAFETY CALL	ENTER
▶▶	
URGENCY CALL	ENTER
▶▶	
GROUP CALL	Channel ENTER
▶▶	
HOME SCREEN	

Log		
LOG VIEW	Previous Next
◀◀	
PREVIOUS ENTRY	Previous Next
▶▶	
NEXT ENTRY	Previous Next

Menu	
MENU 1	Directory Backlight Contrast
MENU 2	Sound MMSI Group
MENU 3	Date/Time Position Channels
MENU 1	

Directory ▶▶	
DIRECTORY OPTIONS	Next Edit Add Delete

Sound ▶▶	
SOUND	Test Distress Test Ring Ring Type

DISTRESS BUTTON	Lift Cover	PRESS and RELEASE	Select Nature of Distress	PRESS and HOLD for 5 Seconds

The Call screens and Menu screens each take a circular form. You can step from one screen to the next, arriving back at the first. References to ENTER on Call screens mean the ENTER key.

14 *Fig 4.2*

DSC Functions

Basic Mode

Fig 4.3 shows the DSC in basic mode with the Home Screen displayed. The equipment is listening for an alert on Ch70; the screen gives time, channel and the position taken from the GPS. The main menu and the log of incoming calls is accessed from this screen.

Fig 4.3

Menu 1 *(see Fig 4.2)*   *Menu 2*   *Menu 3*

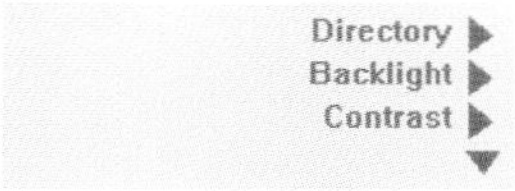

Directory ▶	Sound ▶	Date and Time ▶
Backlight ▶	MMSI ▶	Manual Position ▶
Contrast ▶	Group ▶	Channels ▶
▼	▼	▼

Fig 4.4   *Fig 4.5* 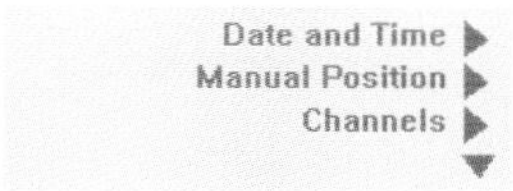   *Fig 4.6*

Incoming routine calls

This routine incoming call is from a UK Ship Station.

The call is acknowledged digitally when the top button is pressed. Voice communication can then begin.

If the name of the calling vessel is stored in the directory, both the name and MMSI would be shown.

Fig 4.7

Editing the directory

The directory may be amended using the alpha-numeric keypad. Programming is similar to a mobile phone.

Entering Group MMSI

The black line shows a group number that has just been entered into the group directory using the keypad. Note that this make of equipment always pre-enters the initial zero.

Fig 4.8

NAVTEX

NAVTEX

Navtex is a component part of the GMDSS. Search and Rescue information together with navigational warnings, gale warnings and weather forecasts are sent at regular intervals from a series of transmitters positioned round the globe. All Navtex receivers use 518KHz, medium frequency, to receive information in English. More advanced equipment is also fitted with 490 KHz to receive additional information in the local language. In the UK, 490 KHz is used for the Inshore Waters Forecast and the extended outlook. Depending on conditions, signals can be received at distances of up to 300 miles and the data can either be printed or shown on a digital display similar to the one shown in Figure 5.1. The special antenna, also shown in Fig 5.1, should be mounted low down away from damage.

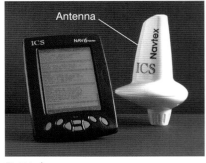

Fig 5.1

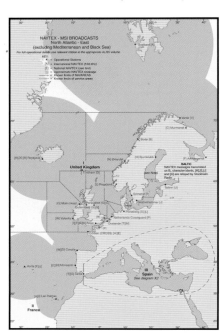

Fig 5.2

Fig 5.2 shows the location of Navtex stations in Western Europe and The Mediterranean. To avoid interference between stations using the same frequency they are each given a time slot for transmission. Each station has an identity letter (Fig 5.3) and the receiver can be programmed to accept only those of interest - if you are sailing off the English coast you may not wish to receive Dutch or French stations within range. The messages are divided into categories (Fig 5.4) and given identity letters so the user can also exclude unwanted messages such as ice alerts and Loran C.

Navtex coverage abroad

Selected Navtex Stations in Metareas I to III, with their identity codes and transmission times are listed below. Times of weather messages are shown in bold. Gale warnings are usually transmitted every 4 hours. Some Navtex receivers can be interfaced with GPS to print out the ship's position at a selected interval, say hourly. Very useful, when all the crew are needed on deck as the log is due to be read.

METAREA I (Co-ordinator – UK)	Transmission times (UT)					
K - **Niton** (Note 1)	0140	0540	0940	1340	1740	2140
L - **Rogoland,** Norway	**0150**	0550	0950	**1350**	1750	2150
L - **Pinneberg,** Hamburg (Note 5)	0150	**0550**	0950	**1350**	1750	**2150**
M - **Oostende,** Belgium (Note 2)	0200	0600	1000	1400	1800	2200
P - **Netherlands CG,** Den Helder	**0230**	0630	1030	1430	1830	2230
S - **Malin Head,** Ireland	0240	**0640**	**1040**	1440	**1840**	**2240**
S - **Pinneberg,** Hamburg (Note 6)	**0300**	**0700**	**1100**	**1500**	**1900**	**2300**
T - **Oostende,** Belgium (Note 3)	0310	**0710**	1110	1510	**1910**	2310
T - **Niton** (Note 4)	0310	**0710**	1110	1510	**1910**	2310
W - **Valentia,** Ireland	0340	**0740**	**1140**	1540	**1940**	**2340**

Notes
1 In English, no weather; only Nav warnings for the French coast from Cap Gris Nez to Île de Brehat
2 No weather information, only Nav warnings for Navarea Juliet.
3 Forecasts and strong wind warnings for Thames and Dover, plus nav info for the Belgium coast.
4 In French, weather info (and Nav warnings) for sea areas Humber to Ouessant (Plymouth)
5 In German, weather and Nav warnings for German Bight (also W & S Baltic at times in bold above)
6 Weather broadcasts every 4 hours for the North Sea

METAREA II (Co-ordinator – France)	Transmission times (UT)					
A - **Corsen,** Le Stiff, France	**0000**	0400	0800	**1200**	1600	2000
D - **Coruña,** Spain	0030	0430	**0830**	1230	1630	**2030**
E - **Corsen,** Le Stiff, France (in French)	0040	0440	**0840**	1240	1640	2040
F - **Horta,** Azores, Portugal	**0050**	0450	**0850**	**1250**	**1650**	**2050**
G - **Monsanto** (in Portuguese)	**0100**	0500	0900	**1300**	1700	2100
G - **Tarifa,** Spain (English & Spanish)	0100	0500	**0900**	1300	1700	**2100**
I - **Las Palmas,** Islas Canarias, Spain	0129	0520	**0920**	1320	**1720**	2120
J - **Horta,** Azores, (in Portuguese)	**0130**	0530	**0930**	1330	**1730**	2130
R - **Monsanto,** Portugal	**0250**	0650	**1050**	1450	**1850**	2250
T - **Tarifa,** Spain (in Spanish)	0310	**0710**	1110	1510	**1910**	2310
W - **Coruña,** Spain (in Spanish)	0340	0740	**1140**	1540	**1940**	2340

METAREA III (Co-ordinator – Spain)	Transmission times (UT)					
M - **Valencia,** Spain (in Spanish)	0200	0600	**1000**	1400	**1800**	2200
S - **La Garde,** Toulon, France (in French)	0300	**0700**	1100	1500	**1900**	2300
W - **La Garde,** Toulon, France	0340	0740	**1140**	1540	1940	**2340**
X - **Valencia,** Spain (English & Spanish)	0350	**0750**	1150	1550	**1950**	2350

Fig 5.3

Navtex Message Categories

A* Navigational warnings
B* Meteorological warnings
C Ice reports
D SAR info and Piracy attack warnings
E Weather forecasts
F Pilot service
H Loran-C
J Satellite navigation
K Other electronic Navaids

L Subfacts and Gunfacts for the UK
V Amplifying navigation warnings initially sent under A; plus weekly oil and gas rig moves
W-Y Special service - trial allocation
Z No messages on hand at scheduled time
G-I and **M-U** are not at present allocated

* These categories cannot be rejected by the receiver.

17

Fig 5.4

EMERGENCY RADIO EQUIPMENT

EMERGENCY POSITION INDICATING RADIO BEACONS (EPIRBs)

An EPIRB is portable, battery operated, waterproof and buoyant. It transmits a distress alert and allows Search and Rescue (SAR) organisations to pinpoint the position of survivors.

For all practical purposes there are three types of EPIRB available to the small boat owner. (The 1.6 GHz INMARSAT and the VHF 121.5 MHz PLBs are outside the scope of this book)

406.025MHz with 121.5MHz

The 406 (*Fig.6.1*) is useful to anyone venturing offshore. The Search and Rescue Satellites listen to and store the emergency message until they are over a ground station, making it possible to provide worldwide coverage. The 406 also has an embedded code which contains the vessel's identification number. The precision and power of the transmitted signal, which includes 121.5MHz as a homing device, allows the satellite to calculate the position of the beacon to within a two-mile radius.

406.025MHz with GPS

A 406MHz EPIRB (*Fig 6.2*) has been designed with an integral miniature GPS which transmits current position and further enhances its lifesaving capabilities. When the beacon is activated this positional information is incorporated into the distress message it transmits. GPS EPIRBs can fix the position to within 25 metres, a great improvement in accuracy.

Fig 6.1

When installing a 406MHz EPIRB it is a legal requirement to inform Falmouth Coastguard of the beacon identity and details of the craft in which it is fitted. This information can be given on the Ship Licence application form.

Careful thought must be given to the installation of the EPIRB. It may be on deck attached by hydrostatic release or stored in a "grab bag". In either case it must be protected from accidental release and inquisitive fingers. If it is accidentally activated you must inform the nearest Coastguard as soon as possible giving details of the beacon and await permission to switch off. This must not be done until the rescue authorities have been contacted, otherwise a search may continue for many hours to locate the source of the transmission.

Fig 6.2

SEARCH AND RESCUE TRANSPONDER (SART)

The SART is a small battery operated beacon (*Fig 6.3*) that produces a distinctive echo on any 3cm radar display. Activated in a small liferaft, surface rescue craft will pick up a contact about five miles away and an aircraft flying at 3000 feet at up to 30 miles. It is used as a homing aid for SAR organisations rather than a means of providing an initial alert so can be considered as complementary to an EPIRB. The battery life is about 96 hours.

If the SART is switched on by accident you must inform the Coastguard without delay in case a passing ship has observed the transponder echo and commenced a search.

Fig 6.3

Fig 6.4

MOBILE PHONES

Most mobile phone networks are designed for use on land but they can give coverage of up to five miles or more in coastal waters. A mobile phone can be a useful means of communicating from on board now that UK Coast Radio Stations no longer offer a ship to shore link call service.

Within the coverage area it can be used to alert the emergency services, including the Coastguard (999/112). However, it cannot perform many of the functions of a marine band radio, such as monitoring a distress frequency. It can only communicate with a single station so calls can't be heard by nearby craft who may be able to assist, and the rescue services cannot accurately direction find from the signal. For these reasons reliance on a mobile phone is not advisable.

USING THE RADIO

English was chosen as the international radio language over one hundred years ago.

Radio channels should never be used for "social chatter". All conversations – called "traffic" - should be about the safety or the manoeuvring of a boat so that vital distress and urgency messages are not missed. The mobile phone should be used to discuss football scores or the local restaurant's menu!

THE RADIO REGULATIONS

The International Telecommunication Union gives the following list of "strictly forbidden transmissions" so that interference is not caused to others.

1. The transmission of profane, indecent or obscene language.

2. Making unnecessary transmissions or transmitting superfluous signals. (This includes whistling into the microphone or discussing the football results!)

3. Transmissions made without identification - the boat's name must be stated every time the microphone is keyed.

4. The broadcast of music.

5. The transmission of false or deceptive distress, safety or identification signals.

6. Transmissions not authorised by the skipper or person in charge of the boat.

7. Operation of the radio by an unauthorised person. Passengers or other members of the crew may make radio telephone calls under the supervision of a qualified operator.

8. The broadcast of messages to an unlicensed shore station. (If you have a VHF scanner at home you may not "broadcast" to your wife that you will be home for tea at 1600!).

9. The use of personal names or unauthorised names in lieu of the boat's name.

10. Closing down the radio before finishing all operations resulting from a distress call.

    (If you have been involved in the rescue of a casualty, you must not shut the radio down until the Coastguard stands you down).

11. The use of frequencies or channels other than those covered by the ship's licence.

SECRECY OF CORRESPONDENCE

Anyone who becomes acquainted with the content of radio telephone calls is legally bound to preserve the secrecy of correspondence and not to "improperly divulge" the contents or even the existence of, correspondence transmitted, received or intercepted.

CONTROL OF COMMUNICATION

Officially it is the station being called who controls communication. However, when DSC is being used it is the caller who chooses the channel. Of course, the called station may always suggest a change of channel if it thinks it necessary.

When DSC is not used it is still preferable for the caller to choose a known empty channel so that the time spent talking on Channel 16 is reduced to a minimum. In all cases a Coast Station controls communication.

GETTING READY TO MAKE A ROUTINE CALL (without DSC)

1. Turn the set on and adjust the squelch.
2. Adjust the volume and select LOW POWER.
3. Select Channel 16.
4. Before transmitting, check that other people are not using the chosen channel. If it is occupied, wait for the end of the conversation or find another channel.
5. Hold the microphone about eight centimetres from the mouth then press the switch on the microphone to transmit - do not speak until you have pressed the button.
6. Prepare to speak clearly and slowly at a normal conversation level. If somebody is likely to write your message down, slow down even more.
7. Try to avoid dropping the voice at the end of a word or phrase. If you have a strong accent, try to make your pronunciation as clear as possible.

HOW TO CALL

First, you must decide how many times you are going to call the other station's name. The general rule is:

Calling another ship station

1. Say their name twice if they are likely to be near the radio but if the weather is bad and the wind is howling it may be prudent to call three times - the Rules states that the maximum is three times.
2. Say your name twice or three times as necessary.

Example call on Ch16:

Seaspray, Seaspray, this is Blue Dolphin, Blue Dolphin. Suggest channel zero eight. Over.

Answer: *Blue Dolphin, this is Seaspray. Switching to channel zero eight.*

Both boats allow time for switching channels then Blue Dolphin makes the first call on Ch8.

Seaspray, this is Blue Dolphin on Ch8. Over

Answer: *Blue Dolphin, Seaspray. Pass your message. Over…*

Calling a marina

1. Select the working channel of the marina (normally Ch80 in the UK) then say their name just once as they are usually listening for calls.
2. Say your own ship's name twice.

Example:

Mercury Marina this is Motor Yacht Blue Dolphin, Blue Dolphin. Over.

Answer: *Blue Dolphin, this is Mercury. What can I do for you? Over.*

Mercury, Blue Dolphin, request a berth for one night for a twelve-metre motor yacht. Over…

UNANSWERED CALLS

If you have made a routine call to another ship station and receive no reply, check that the volume and the squelch control are set correctly and that you are tuned to an appropriate channel. Turn to high power.

In any event, you must wait for at least TWO minutes before calling again. You are permitted to call 3 times at two-minute intervals after which you must wait 3 minutes before trying again. As a rule, if another boat has not answered you after two calls, he is probably not listening – do not call again.

THE PHONETIC ALPHABET

Is understood internationally and may be used when a difficult word or group of letters have to be spelt out. This phonetic alphabet is shown in Annex A (page 34).

Before a word is spelt, the words "*I Spell*" should be used.

Example:

"*Intend to anchor off Youghal – I spell – Yankee Oscar Uniform Golf Hotel Alfa Lima –Youghal*".

If a Coastguard asks for your international call sign, which is MBDD, you would transmit:

My call sign is Mike Bravo Delta Delta.

PHONETIC NUMERALS

The phonetic pronunciation of numerals, shown at Annex A, should be used when numerals are transmitted.

PROCEDURE WORDS (PROWORDS)

Prowords might be described as those the professionals use. All are designed for easy international understanding and brevity. Not included are rambling pieces of chat such as:

"I am signing off this channel now but will listen for any further communication from you. Have a good day!"

The Standard Marine Navigational Vocabulary was compiled to standardise communication for navigation at sea, in harbours, estuaries and port approaches and is published in full in Merchant Shipping Notice M1252, which may be obtained from the MCA web site www.mcga.gov.uk.

Shown below are the words that candidates for the SRC examination need to know.

THIS IS – From a station whose name or callsign immediately follows.

OVER – The invitation to reply. "Over and Out" is NEVER used.

OUT – This is said by each station at the end of working.

REQUEST RADIO CHECK – Please tell me the strength and clarity of my transmission.

I SAY AGAIN – I am repeating what I have just said (or a portion of it).

STATION CALLING – Used when a station receives a call which is intended for it but is uncertain of the identification of the calling station.

READ BACK – Please read back the message that I have just sent to you.

WRONG – Reply to a message that has just been "read back" but is in error.

CORRECT – Reply to a message that has been read back for check.

CORRECTION – Spoken when a mistake has been made. The correct words or group follows.

RECEIVED – Your message has been received and understood. In case of language difficulties the word ROMEO may be used (NOT Roger).

WAIT – If a station is unable to accept traffic immediately, it will reply with the words Wait... minutes.

I SPELL – I shall spell the next word or group.

ALL AFTER – Used after the pro-words "Say again" to request the repetition of a portion of a list or message.

ALL BEFORE – Used after the pro-words "Say again" to request the repetition of a portion of a list or message.

REPEAT – Used if any part of a message is considered important to need emphasing.

Example: *My intended berth is Delta three zero – repeat – Delta three zero. Over.*

POSITION

When latitude and longitude are used these shall be expressed in degrees and minutes (and decimals of a minute if necessary) North or South of the Equator and East or West of Greenwich.

The numerals should be spoken digit by digit.

Example: **50° 12'.4N 001° 27'.7W** should be read:

Five zero degrees one two decimal four minutes north, zero zero one degrees two seven decimal seven minutes west.

When the position is related to a mark, it should be a well-defined charted object. The bearing should in the 360° notation from True North and be that of the position FROM the mark.

Example:

"My position is one eight zero degrees from Portland Bill Lighthouse two decimal four miles."

DISTANCES

Preferably to be expressed in nautical miles or cables (tenths of a mile). Metres and kilometres may be used but the unit used should always be stated.

SPEED

To be expressed in knots. Without further notation meaning **speed through the water**.

TIME

Use the 24-hour clock and indicate whether it is UTC (Universal time), local time or zone time.

GARBLED CALLS

When a station receives a call but is uncertain for whom it is intended.

Example: *…this is Born Free – over*

It must not reply until the call has been repeated and understood.

UNKNOWN CALLING STATION

When a station receives a call intended for it but is uncertain of the name of the calling station, it should reply:

Station calling Barbican –This is Barbican – say again – over.

USE OF THE RADIOTELEPHONE WHEN IN PORT

Generally a radiotelephone may be used only for port operations and on private channels (e.g. Ch M2) when in UK harbours and estuaries. Use the mobile phone to talk to another boat in the marina – not the VHF radio.

DISTRESS PROCEDURES

DEFINITION OF DISTRESS

The definition of distress in the 1979 Search and Rescue Convention is:

Grave and Imminent Danger to a Person, Ship, Aircraft or Other Vehicle Requiring Immediate Assistance.

DISTRESS is announced using the word MAYDAY, derived from the French 'M'aidez', meaning 'Help me'. This prefix must only be used for distress traffic and, except in a distress situation, the word MAYDAY should never be used on the radio even in conversation.

Emergencies that do not fall into the distress category but where an urgent message needs to be passed concerning the safety of a person, ship, aircraft or other vehicle, are URGENCY messages prefixed PAN-PAN.

Transmissions concerning the safety of navigation are prefixed SÉCURITÉ.

Urgency and Safety are covered on pages 29-31.

DISTRESS TRANSMISSION

There are three separate parts to a distress transmission:

A. The DSC Distress Alert
B. The Voice Distress Call
C. The Voice Distress Message

Parts A, B and C are used if DSC is fitted. Parts B and C if it is not.

To send a distress alert

Fig 8.1 shows the display after one press of the RED button and selection of the nature of distress

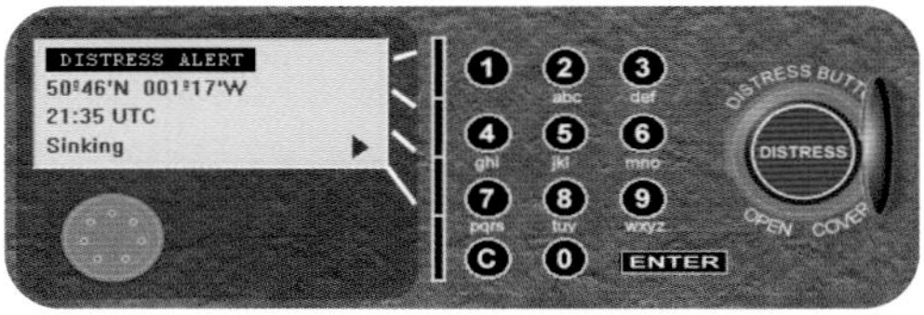

Fig 8.1

To send a distress alert from the DSC you should:

1. Lift the cover of the RED distress button.

2. Press the RED distress button momentarily.

3. Select the Nature of Distress if time allows i.e. fire, sinking, collision etc.

4. Depress the RED button for five seconds or until the apparatus informs you that the alert has been sent.

    The equipment will now automatically send a short electronic data burst on Ch70 giving:
    a) your MMSI
    b) your position (from GPS or manual entry)
    c) time the distress alert was sent
    d) the nature of distress (if selected)

5. The screen will indicate Ch16 - it is automatically tuned in preparation for voice communication. The whole process takes about 15 seconds.

6. The VHF DSC apparatus will repeat the distress alert approximately every four minutes until a digital acknowledgement is received on Ch70 or until the originating station cancels the alert. The screen will display the MMSI of the acknowledging station.

7. Wait 15 seconds and then give the voice Distress Call and Message.

24

The distress call

A distress call has absolute priority over all other transmissions. All stations hearing it must immediately cease any transmissions which could cause interference to the distress traffic. They must then continue to listen on the frequency for the distress message.

Mayday, Mayday, Mayday
This is Yacht Calamity, Calamity, Calamity. MMSI (or call-sign if no DSC fitted)

The distress message

The distress message follows the distress call without a break and should be spoken SLOWLY and CLEARLY. Remember that your rescuer will be trying to write down your position and other details. The internationally recognised format is:

Mayday Yacht Calamity
Position (in Lat and Long or a true bearing and distance from a prominent charted object)
Nature of distress (fire, sinking, hit a submerged object etc.)
Assistance required
Total number of persons on board (important as it could affect the choice of rescue method)
Other useful information (anything that may assist the rescuer eg: taking to liferaft, person injured, etc.)
Over (awaiting a reply)

The following is an example of a complete voice distress transmission following a DSC distress alert:

Mayday, Mayday, Mayday
This is Yacht Calamity, Calamity, Calamity MMSI 234001234
Mayday Yacht Calamity
My position is 50° 46'N 001° 17'W
Swamped in rough sea and sinking
I require immediate assistance
Five people on board
Abandoning to liferaft
Over

Fig 8.2 Awaiting a digital DSC response

Fig 8.3 Display in receiving vessel

EMERGENCY PROCEDURE CARDS

It is strongly recommended that an emergency procedure card is affixed to a bulkhead close to the radio set. Copies of suitable cards are shown at Annex B on pages 36 & 37.

DISTRESS REPLY

In (*Fig 8.4*) Solent Coastguard has given a digital response. Stand by for a voice message.

Fig 8.4

Having sent the distress message you should receive an immediate reply from the Coastguard or other shore authority, or in mid-ocean from any ship receiving. Those fitted with DSC will receive a digital response before the voice acknowledgement.

The voice format is:

Mayday Yacht Calamity, Calamity, Calamity   MMSI 234001234 (if fitted with DSC)
This is Solent Coastguard, Solent Coastguard, Solent Coastguard
Received Mayday
Launching SAR Helicopter
Standby

RECEIVING A DISTRESS MESSAGE

The International Regulations state, 'The obligation to accept Distress calls and messages is absolute in the case of every station without distinction, and such messages must be accepted with priority over all other messages, they must be answered and the necessary steps must immediately be taken to give effect to them.

Class D equipment does not enable you to acknowledge a Mayday digitally or to switch off the DSC alerting system in another craft; that requires a Coast Station or a vessel fitted with a Class A or B controller. It is likely that a Coast Station will accept responsibility for the rescue within a very short time and is in an ideal position to help with lifeboats, helicopters and medical aid. If you hear a Distress Alert and message you should:

1) write down all the distress information and inform your skipper
2) wait a short time to see if a Coast Station acknowledges

If there is no reply to the message after four minutes and the Distress Alert is repeated, you should attempt to send a MAYDAY RELAY. If that's impossible and you have still not heard an acknowledgement then you must send a voice RECEIVED MAYDAY message and proceed to the vessel in distress, while continuing to repeat the Mayday Relay message.

Note that you won't receive a Distress Alert if you are transmitting on VHF when it's sent, because the equipment can either receive or transmit - not both at the same time. This is one reason why the Alert is repeated at four-minute intervals.

Mayday relay procedure

A ship or shore station that learns of a vessel in distress should transmit a Mayday Relay call and message when:

a) the station in distress cannot itself transmit a distress message.
b) sighting a non-radio distress signal (flares, fire, flags or shapes).
c) although not in a position to render assistance, she has heard a distress message which has not been acknowledged.

When a station, not herself in distress, is transmitting a Mayday Relay this fact must be made quite clear. If this is not done, direction-finding bearings might be taken on the Station transmitting the relay and assistance could be directed to the wrong position.

Using DSC to send a Mayday Relay

The Class D VHF DSC has no facility for sending a Mayday Relay Alert so an URGENCY ALERT should be transmitted (see Page 29). This doesn't include a position and won't confuse the situation but it will alert other stations and automatically switch their VHF to Ch16 ready for your Mayday Relay Call and Message.

The Mayday Relay Call and message

The Mayday Relay Call and message are formatted as follows:

Mayday Relay (repeated three times)
This is (name or callsign of the station making the transmission, spoken three times)
Mayday (Name and MMSI of vessel in distress)
Nature of the distress
Assistance required
Time (optional)
Over

For example, Motor Yacht *Bluebell* has heard a Mayday message from the Yacht *Calamity*. No one has acknowledged after five minutes. *Bluebell* sends a DSC Urgency Alert and then gives the voice follow up on Ch16:

Mayday Relay, Mayday Relay, Mayday Relay
This is Motor Yacht Bluebell, Bluebell, Bluebell, MMSI 233000285
Mayday Yacht Calamity MMSI 234001526
Position 50° 46'N 001° 17'W
Swamped in rough sea and sinking
Require immediate assistance
Five persons on board
Abandoning to liferaft
Over

IMPOSING RADIO SILENCE

The station controlling distress traffic may impose silence. To achieve this it transmits:

Mayday
All Stations, All Stations, All Stations
This is Solent Coastguard, Solent Coastguard, Solent Coastguard
Mayday Calamity
Seelonce Mayday
Time 2144 UTC
Out

The expression **Seelonce Mayday** is reserved for the use of the station controlling distress traffic or the casualty. No other station may use it.

If any other station close to the incident believes it essential it may also impose silence, but in this case it must use the expression **Seelonce Distress.**

All stations aware of, but not taking part in, distress traffic are forbidden to transmit on the channel being used for distress.

Relaxing radio silence

When distress traffic is being handled on Ch16 all normal communication on the frequency is suspended. As it is also the international calling frequency, delays in normal traffic are inevitable.

When complete silence is no longer considered necessary, the station controlling distress traffic will indicate on Ch16 that restricted working may be resumed for urgent traffic. The word **Prudence** is used as in the following example:

Mayday
All Stations, All Stations, All Stations
This is Belfast Coastguard, Belfast Coastguard, Belfast Coastguard
Mayday Eclipse
Prudonce, Prudonce
Time 0345 UTC
Out

Cancelling radio silence

When the distress traffic has completely ceased, the station which has controlled the distress traffic must let all stations know that normal working may be resumed. This is done using the expression: **Seelonce Feenee**. For example:

Mayday
All Stations, All Stations, All Stations
This is Dover Coastguard, Dover Coastguard, Dover Coastguard
Mayday Yacht Calamity

Seelonce Feenee
Time 1045 UTC
Out

DIRECTION FINDING

Lifeboats and some Search and Rescue (SAR) aircraft are fitted with direction finding (D/F) receivers and may request a yacht in distress to transmit a signal suitable for direction finding.

A lifeboat wishing to take a D/F bearing would transmit:

Mayday Yacht Blaze
This is Portland Lifeboat
For direction finding purposes request you hold your Press to Transmit button closed for a period of ten seconds followed by your name
Repeat this three times on this frequency
Over

The reply should be:

Mayday
Portland Lifeboat
This is Yacht Blaze
(10 sec transmission)
Yacht Blaze
(This sequence should be repeated 3 times)

As the rescue craft draws closer to the casualty there may be a further request for a transmission.

FALSE ALERTS

Much time and money can be expended searching for a distressed vessel after a false alert. It is essential that the procedure for cancelling a false alert is known and used immediately the mistake is realised.

False VHF DSC distress alert

Allow the alert transmission to complete once. If no aknowledgement is received from another station switch off the DSC equipment to prevent a repeat transmission.
Switch VHF equipment back on and set to Ch16.
Make an All Stations voice broadcast giving ship's name, MMSI and position.
Cancel False Distress and give time.
Confirm that the nearest Coastguard has received your All Stations voice broadcast.
Example:

All Stations, All Stations, All Stations
This is Yacht Dunce, Dunce, Dunce, MMSI 233003765
In position 50° 34'.2 N 002° 28'.1 W
Distress Alert sent in error
Cancel Distress Alert sent at 0245 UTC
Out

406MHz false EPIRB alert

DO NOT switch off the 406 EPIRB beacon.
Report the false alert to the nearest Coastguard, relaying through another station if necessary.
Give the position and serial number of the beacon.
When instructed, switch off the 406 EPIRB.

URGENCY, SAFETY & COASTGUARD LIAISON

URGENCY MESSAGES

Urgency messages are prefixed with the words **PAN-PAN** repeated three times. This indicates that the vessel or crew have a serious problem but are not in a distress situation. It is often difficult to decide whether to send a MAYDAY or PAN-PAN message.

Consider the definition of Distress: ".....Grave and imminent danger and requires IMMEDIATE ASSISTANCE", anything less may justify an urgency signal.

Examples of Urgency include a boat taking on water, but not yet sinking; an engine failure with no other means of propulsion but some distance from a lee shore; injury to a crew member who needs treatment but whose life is not threatened. Remember that an urgency situation can always be upgraded to a distress situation.

Urgency alerting by DSC

Fig 9.1

Using DSC select Urgency Call and press the Enter button (*Fig 9.1*)

Fig 9.2

The equipment will ask for confirmation that an Urgency Call is required. (*Fig 9.2*)

Fig 9.3

Once it has got the confirmation it will then send the alert and the radio will automatically switch to Ch16. (*Fig 9.3*)

On receipt by an operator in another vessel, the audio alarm will sound and the VHF radio will automatically switch to Ch16 (*Fig 9.4*).

All Ships urgency
From 234006016
On 16
6/19:47

Fig 9.4

The visual display will indicate that an Urgency Call has been received and will display the MMSI of the issuing ship station. Unlike Distress, Urgency Alerts do not include the ship's position (even though this may be displayed on the sender's screen) so it is essential that this is included in the voice urgency message.

The urgency call and message

After sending the DSC alert the operator must wait 15 seconds before sending the voice Urgency Call and message on Ch16. Whether DSC is fitted or not, the voice message is almost identical; the only difference is that the MMSI must be given if DSC is present.

It will be seen from the examples below that the message by voice should be addressed to a particular station or stations. This could be to 'All Ships', 'All Stations' or to a local HM Coastguard Station. Note that if an Urgency Alert has been sent by DSC then the vessel's MMSI must be included in the urgency message to enable the alert and the message to be correlated.

Pan-Pan, Pan-Pan, Pan-Pan
All Ships, All Ships, All Ships
This is (Name or callsign three times)
MMSI
Position, (either lat and long or bearing and distance FROM a charted object)
Nature of urgency
Assistance required
Number of persons on board
Other useful information to assist
Over

An example of such a message is as follows:

Pan-Pan, Pan-Pan, Pan-Pan
Falmouth Coastguard, Falmouth Coastguard, Falmouth Coastguard
This is Motor Yacht Unfortunate, Unfortunate, Unfortunate. MMSI 234001546
My position is 49° 38'.45N 006° 20'.14W
Total engine failure and drifting,
I require assistance to clear Traffic Separation Scheme
Two persons on board
Colour of hull black, upperwork white
Over

The nearest Coast Station will normally acknowledge a DSC Urgency Alert and message by voice provided that it is in VHF range. The Coastguard may also repeat the PAN-PAN message on Ch16 after which he will take control of further traffic.

SAFETY

The proword for Safety messages is **Sécurité** (French again), pronounced **'say-cure-ee-tay'**.

This word is spoken three times indicating that the station is about to transmit a message containing an important navigational or meteorological warning. It normally originates from a shore authority but may, under special circumstances, be sent by a vessel at sea. This will be a rare event and only likely if you were to sight something like a partly submerged container in an area of high density traffic.

The DSC safety alert

Select Safety Call from the call menu.

Now press the Enter button. The equipment will ask for confirmation that you wish to send a safety alert (*Fig 9.5*) and, when confirmed, will send the alert. Your VHF radio will automatically switch to Ch16.

Fig 9.5

The Safety Alert is less strident than Distress and Urgency. It will be heard on a receiving vessel and by the Coastguard, their visual displays indicating that a Safety Alert has been received. Receiving stations should be prepared to write down any subsequent message.

The safety call

A Safety Call, given by voice on Ch16 will announce which working channel is to be used for the main body of the message.

Example: on Ch16

Sécurité, Sécurité, Sécurité
All Stations, All Stations, All Stations
This is Humber Coastguard, Humber Coastguard, Humber Coastguard
For urgent navigational warning listen Channel 67
Out

Then on Ch67

Sécurité, Sécurité, Sécurité
All Stations, All Stations, All Stations
This is Humber Coastguard, Humber Coastguard, Humber Coastguard
Large drifting hulk reported in position five one degrees four zero minutes North, one degree one zero minutes East
Considered to be a danger to surface navigation
Time of origin one two three zero UTC
Out

All stations hearing the safety call on Ch16 should switch to the working channel (Ch67). They must listen to the message until they are satisfied that it is of no concern to them. They must not make any transmission likely to interfere with the message.

COASTGUARD LIAISON

Calling the Coastguard

All HM Coastguard Rescue Centres keep a constant watch on VHF DSC Ch70 and 16. Ch67 is available in the UK for use by small craft for the exchange of SAFETY information in situations which do not justify the use of distress or urgency procedures.

Urgent medical advice can be obtained through any UK HM Coastguard Maritime Rescue Centre by using a DSC URGENCY ALERT. The voice follow-up on Ch16 should be prefixed with the words PAN-PAN spoken three times. The call and message follows the same format as the Urgency call shown earlier in this chapter.

The Coastguard encourages skippers of small craft on longer passages to pass safety information; who you are and where you are going. However HMCG has neither the facilities nor the manpower to continually track a yacht's progress from port to port and they won't initiate a search unless your shore-side contact informs them that you are overdue.

MARITIME SAFETY INFORMATION BROADCASTS (MSI)

As soon as a Gale or Strong Wind warning is issued an announcement is made on Channel 16. This will direct listeners to a working channel, typically channels 23,84 or 86. Routine weather information broadcasts are made three-hourly with a new forecast every six hours.

The full broadcast referred to in the table contains:

Shipping forecast, new Inshore Waters forecast, 24 hour outlook, Gale and Strong Wind warnings, Navigational warnings and Fishermen's 3 day forecast, Subfacts & Gunfacts (where appropriate)

COASTGUARD	3 hourly (local time) from	FULL BROADCAST	INSHORE WATERS AREAS
Falmouth & Brixham	0110	0710 & 1910	Land's End to St David's Head inc Bristol Channel. Lyme Regis to Land's End inc Isles of Scilly
Portland & Solent	0130	0730 & 1930	Selsey Bill to Lyme Regis
Dover & Thames	0110	0710 & 1910	Gibraltar Point to North Foreland North Foreland to Selsey Bill
Yarmouth	0150	0750 & 1950	Whitby to Gibraltar Point Gibraltar Point to North Foreland
Humber	0150	0750 & 1950	Berwick on Tweed to Whitby Whitby to Gibraltar Point
Forth & Aberdeen	0130	0730 & 1930	Cape Wrath to Rattray Head inc Orkney Rattray Head to Berwick on Tweed
Shetland	0110	0710 & 1910	Cape Wrath to Rattray Head inc Orkney Shetland Isles within 60 miles of Lerwick
Stornoway	0110	0710 & 1910	Ardnamurchan Pt. to Cape Wrath inc Outer Hebrides
Clyde	0210	0810 & 2010	Mull of Galloway to Mull of Kintrye inc Firth of Clyde & North Channel Mull of Kintyre to Ardnamurchan Point
Belfast	0110	0710 & 1910	Lough Foyle to Carlingford Lough, Isle of Man Mull of Galloway to Mull of Kintyre inc Firth of Clyde & North Channel
Liverpool	0130	0730 & 1930	Great Orme Head to the Mull of Galloway Isle of Man
Holyhead	0150	0750 & 1950	St David's Head to Great Orme Head Great Orme Head to the Mull of Galloway
Milford Haven & Swansea	0150	0750 & 1950	Land's End to St David's Head inc Bristol Channel. St David's Head to Great Orme Head

Details of European shore stations issuing meteorological bulletins at fixed times are published in nautical almanacs.

VHF direction finding

A number of Coastguard Stations can obtain a radio bearing from a Ch16 transmission. Simultaneous bearings from two or more Coastguard aerial sites will provide a position fix. The primary purpose is to assist in the rescue of casualties but the Coastguard may be able to provide such information to a yachtsman who is concerned about his position. It should be stressed that this is not an entitlement but a bonus if it happens to be available.

In other European countries Rescue Centres use different working channels and you are advised to consult a nautical almanac for the relevant information.

ANNEX A - PHONETIC ALPHABET & FIGURE-SPELLING TABLES

PHONETIC ALPHABET		
Letter	**Word**	**Pronounced as**
A	Alfa	<u>AL</u> FAH
B	Bravo	<u>BRAH</u> VOH
C	Charlie	<u>CHAR</u> LEE or <u>SHAR</u> LEE
D	Delta	<u>DELL</u> TAH
E	Echo	<u>ECK</u> OH
F	Foxtrot	<u>FOKS</u> TROT
G	Golf	GOLF
H	Hotel	HOH <u>TELL</u>
I	India	<u>IN</u> DEE AH
J	Juliet	<u>JEW</u> LEE <u>ETT</u>
K	Kilo	KEY LOH
L	Lima	LEE MAH
M	Mike	MIKE
N	November	NO <u>VEM</u> BER
O	Oscar	<u>OSS</u> CAH
P	Papa	PAH PAH
Q	Quebec	KEH <u>BECK</u>
R	Romeo	<u>ROW</u> ME OH
S	Sierra	SEE <u>AIR</u> RAH
T	Tango	<u>TANG</u> GO
U	Uniform	<u>YOU</u> NEE FORM or <u>OO</u> NEE FORM
V	Victor	<u>VIK</u> TAH
W	Whiskey	<u>WISS</u> KEY
X	X-ray	<u>ECKS</u> RAY
Y	Yankee	<u>YANG</u> KEY
Z	Zulu	<u>ZOO</u> LOO

Note: The syllables to be emphasised are underlined

When numerals are transmitted by radiotelephone, the following rules for their pronunciation should be observed.

PHONETIC NUMERALS	
Numeral	**Spoken as**
1	WUN
2	TOO
3	TREE
4	FOW-ER
5	FIFE
6	SIX
7	SEV-EN
8	AIT
9	NIN-ER
0	ZERO

Numerals should be transmitted digit by digit except that multiples of thousands may be spoken as such.

Numeral	Spoken as
44	FOW-ER FOW-ER
90	NIN-ER ZERO
1478	WUN FOW-ER SEV-EN AIT
7000	SEV-EN THOUSAND
136	WUN TREE SIX
500	FIFE ZERO ZERO

DISTRESS PROCEDURE - Card 1

The following procedure card should be displayed in full view of the VHF radio installation (as per instructions given in M Notice 1646).

This Distress Procedure card is for vessels FITTED WITH DIGITAL SELECTIVE CALLING. The words printed in bold type should be highlighted in **RED**.

DISTRESS PROCEDURE

Name of Vessel ....….............. MMSI ....…............Callsign ....

DISTRESS ALERTS are to be made only when **IMMEDIATE ASSISTANCE IS REQUIRED**

What you must do:

Check that the main battery is switched on

Switch on the VHF/DSC

Open the cover to the **RED** distress button

Press the **RED** button once

If time permits select DISTRESS TYPE i.e. SINKING, FIRE etc.

Press and hold the **RED** button down for 5 seconds

Wait for 15 seconds then **DEPRESS THE TRANSMIT BUTTON** on the hand microphone.

Speaking <u>SLOWLY</u> and <u>CLEARLY</u> into the microphone SAY:

MAYDAY, MAYDAY, MAYDAY

THIS IS   (Repeat name of vessel three times)

MMSI   (See above)

MAYDAY   (Name of vessel spoken once)

MY POSITION IS   (Latitude and Longitude or True bearing and distance from a charted feature)

NATURE OF DISTRESS   (e.g. sinking, on fire, etc)

I REQUIRE IMMEDIATE ASSISTANCE

NUMBER OF PERSONS ON BOARD and OTHER USEFUL INFORMATION

OVER

Release the transmit button and wait for an acknowledgement

Keep listening on Ch16 for instructions

If an acknowledgement is not received repeat the voice distress call and message

MIRPDANIO

ANNEX B - DISTRESS PROCEDURE - Card 2

The following procedure card should be displayed in full view of the VHF radio installation. (as per instructions given in M Notice 1646).

This version is for vessels <u>NOT</u> FITTED WITH DIGITAL SELECTIVE CALLING. The words printed in bold type should be highlighted in **RED**

DISTRESS PROCEDURE

Name of Vessel ………………….........…..…………. Callsign …………………….........……..

DISTRESS CALLS are to be made only when **IMMEDIATE ASSISTANCE IS REQUIRED**

What you must do:

Check that the main battery is switched on

Switch on the VHF. Check Ch16 25W is selected

DEPRESS THE TRANSMIT BUTTON on the hand microphone.

MAYDAY, MAYDAY, MAYDAY

THIS IS   (Repeat name of vessel three times)

CALLSIGN   (See above)

MAYDAY   (Name of vessel spoken once)

MY POSITION IS   (Latitude and Longitude or True bearing
                                                  and distance from a charted feature)

NATURE OF DISTRESS   (e.g. sinking, on fire, etc)

I REQUIRE IMMEDIATE ASSISTANCE

NUMBER OF PERSONS ON BOARD and OTHER USEFUL INFORMATION

OVER

Release the transmit button and wait for an acknowledgement

Keep listening on Ch16 for instructions

If an acknowledgement is not received repeat the voice distress call and message

ANNEX C - VHF FREQUENCIES

INTERNATIONAL VHF FREQUENCIES

Channel Number	Notes	Transmitting Frequency MHz		Intership	Port Operations and Ship Movement		Public Correspondence
		Ship Stations	Coast Stations		Single Frequency	Two Frequency	
60		156.025	160.625			X	X
01		156.050	160.650			X	X
61		156.075	160.675			X	X
02		156.100	160.700			X	X
62		156.125	160.725			X	X
03		156.150	160.750			X	X
63		156.175	160.775			X	X
04		156.200	160.800			X	X
64		156.225	160.825			X	X
05		156.250	160.850			X	X
65		156.275	160.875			X	X
06		156.300	156.300	X	X		
66		156.325	160.925			X	X
07		156.350	160.950			X	X
67		156.375	156.375	Small Ship Safety Channel			
08		156.400	156.400	X	X		
68		156.425	156.425		X		
09	1	156.450	156.450	X	X		
69	1	156.475	156.475	X	X		
10	1, 4	156.500	156.500	X	X		
70	3	156.525	156.525	Digital Selective Calling Only			
11		156.550	156.550		X		
71		156.575	156.575		X		
12		156.600	156.600		X		
72		156.625	156.625	X	X		
13	1	156.650	156.650	X	X	Bridge to Bridge Working	
73	1	156.675	156.675	X	X		
14		156.700	156.700		X		
74		156.725	156.725		X		
15	1, 2	156.750	156.750	X	X		

Channel Number	Notes	Transmitting Frequency MHz Ship Stations	Coast Stations	Intership	Port Operations and Ship Movement Single Frequency	Two Frequency	Public Correspondence
75	1, 2	156.775	156.775	X	X		
16		156.800	156.800	Distress Safety and Calling			
76	1, 2	156.825	156.825	X	X		
17	1, 2	156.850	156.850	X	X		
77		156.875	156.875	X	X		
18		156.900	161.500			X	
78		156.925	161.525			X	X
19		156.950	161.550			X	
79		156.975	161.575			X	
20		157.000	161.600			X	
80		157.025	161.625			X	
21		157.050	161.650			X	
81		157.075	161.675			X	X
22		157.100	161.700			X	
82		157.125	161.725			X	X
23	6	157.150	161.750	HM Coastguard Routine Weather & Safety (UK)			
83		157.175	161.775				X
24		157.200	161.800				X
84		157.225	161.825	HM Coastguard Routine Weather & Safety (UK)			
25		157.250	161.850				X
85		157.275	161.875				X
26		157.300	161.900				X
86	6	157.325	161.925	HM Coastguard Routine Weather & Safety (UK)			
27		157.350	161.950				X
87		157.375	161.975				X
28		157.400	161.200				X
88		157.425	162.025				X

Notes:

1. Although there are 11 intership channels listed in this International Agreement, in practice only the channels **NOT** shared with Port Operations should be selected for intership use, ie. 06, 08, 72 and 77.

2. Channels 15, 17, 75 & 76 are restricted to 1 watt, most transmitters will automatically switch to low power when these channels are selected.

3. Channel 70 is reserved for Digital Selective Calling and must **NEVER** be used for voice communication.

4. Channel used for Oil Pollution Control.

5. The Guard Band channels cannot be selected on type approved equipment.

VHF FREQUENCIES USED IN THE USA

Channel Number	Transmitting Frequency MHz		Use
	Ship Stations	Coast Stations	
15	Nil	156.750	Environmental – receive only
	Nil	156.775	Guard Band – Not Used
	Nil	156.825	Guard Band – Not Used
01A	156.050	156.050	Port Operations (Simplex)
63A	156.175	156.175	Port Operations (Simplex)
05A	156.250	156.250	Port Operations (Simplex)
65A	156.275	156.275	Port Operations (Simplex)
06	156.300	156.300	Intership Safety
66A	156.325	156.325	Port Operations (Simplex)
07A	156.350	156.350	Commercial
67	156.375	156.375	Commercial
08	156.400	156.400	Commercial Intership
68	156.425	156.425	Non Commercial
09	156.450	156.450	Boater Calling
69	156.475	156.475	Non Commercial
10	156.500	156.500	Commercial
70	156.525	156.525	Digital Selective Calling Only
11	156.550	156.550	Commercial
71	156.575	156.575	Non Commercial
12	156.600	156.600	Port Operations (Simplex)
72	156.625	156.625	Non Commercial Intership (Simplex)
13	156.650	156.650	Bridge-to-Bridge Safety of Navigation (Simplex)
73	156.675	156.675	Port Operations (Simplex)
14	156.700	156.700	Port Operations (Simplex)
74	156.725	156.725	Port Operations (Simplex)
16	156.800	156.800	Distress, Safety and Calling Only
17	156.850	156.850	State Control
77	156.875	156.875	Port Operations (Simplex)
18A	156.900	156.900	Commercial

Channel Number	Transmitting Frequency MHz		Use
	Ship Stations	Coast Stations	
78A	156.925	156.925	Non Commercial
19A	156.950	156.950	Commercial
79A	156.975	156.975	Commercial
20	157.000	161.600	Port Operations (Duplex)
20A	157.000	157.000	Port Operations (Simplex)
80A	157.025	157.025	Commercial
21A	157.050	157.050	US Coast Guard only
81A	157.075	157.075	US Government – Environmental Protection
22A	157.100	157.100	Coast Guard Liaison
82A	157.125	157.125	US Government only
23A	157.150	157.150	US Coast Guard only
83A	157.175	157.175	US Coast Guard only
24	157.200	161.800	Public Correspondence (Duplex)
84	157.225	161.825	Public Correspondence (Duplex)
25	157.250	161.850	Public Correspondence (Duplex)
85	157.275	161.875	Public Correspondence (Duplex)
26	157.300	161.900	Public Correspondence (Duplex)
86	157.325	161.925	Public Correspondence (Duplex)
27	157.350	161.950	Public Correspondence (Duplex)
87	157.375	161.975	Public Correspondence (Duplex)
28	157.400	162.000	Public Correspondence (Duplex)
88	157.425	162.025	Public Correspondence (Duplex)
88A	157.425	157.425	Commercial Intership (Simplex)

Important Note:

The American frequency plan is included to highlight the differences between the American and International configuration. It would be very unwise for a UK resident to purchase an American VHF radio in the USA for use in the UK; it would not be type approved and would be unable to receive and transmit on many of the international channels.

ANNEX D -
EXTRACTS FROM MARITIME GUIDANCE NOTES

Extract from MARITIME GUIDANCE NOTE MGM 324 (M+F):

Proper Use of VHF Channels at Sea

1. The International Maritime Organisation (IMO) has noted with concern the widespread misuse of VHF channels at sea especially the distress, safety and calling Ch16 (156.8MHz) and 70 (156.525MHz), and channels used for port operations, ship movement services and reporting systems. Although VHF at sea makes an important contribution to navigational safety, its misuse causes serious interference and, in itself, becomes a danger to safety at sea. IMO has asked Member Governments to ensure that VHF channels are used correctly.

2. All users of marine VHF on United Kingdom vessels, and all other vessels in United Kingdom territorial waters and harbours, are therefore reminded, in conformance with international and national legislation, marine VHF apparatus may only be used in accordance with the International Telecommunication Union's (ITU) Radio Regulations. These Regulations specifically prescribe that:

   a) Ch16 may only be used for distress, urgency and very brief safety communications and for calling to establish other communications which should then be concluded on a suitable working channel.

   b) Ch70 may only be used for Digital Selective Calling not oral communication.

   c) On VHF channels allocated to port operations or ship movement services such as VTS, the only messages permitted are restricted to those relating to operational handling, the movement and the safety of ships and to the safety of persons.

   d) All signals must be preceded by an identification, for example the vessel's name or callsign.

   e) The service of every VHF radio telephone station shall be controlled by an operator holding a certificate issued or recognised by the station's controlling administration, normally the vessel's country of registration. Providing the station is so controlled, other persons besides the holder of the certificate may use the equipment.

3. Appendix 1 to this notice consists of notes on guidance on the use of VHF at sea and is an extract from IMO Resolution A.474(XII). Masters, Skippers and Owners are urged to ensure that VHF channels are used in accordance with this guidance.

4. For routine ship-to-ship communications, the following channels have been made available in United Kingdom waters: 6, 8, 72 and 77. Masters, Skippers and Owners are urged to ensure that all ship-to-ship communications working in these waters are confined to these channels, selecting that most appropriate in the local conditions at the time.

5. Channel 13 is designated for use on a world-wide basis as a navigation safety communication channel, primarily for intership navigation safety communications. It may also be used for the ship movement and port services subject to the national regulations of the administrations concerned.

GUIDANCE ON THE USE OF VHF AT SEA

1. Preparation

Before transmitting, think about the subjects which have to be communicated and, if necessary, prepare written notes to avoid unnecessary interruptions and ensure that no valuable time is wasted on a busy channel.

2. Listening

Listen before commencing to transmit to make certain that the channel is not already in use. This will avoid unnecessary and irritating interference.

3. Discipline

VHF equipment should be used correctly and in accordance with the Radio Regulations. The following in particular should be avoided:

a) calling on Channel 16 for purposes other than distress, urgency and very brief safety communications when another calling channel is available;

b) communication on Channel 70 other than for Digital Selective Calling;

c) communications not related to safety and navigation on port operation channels;

d) non-essential transmissions, e.g. needless and superfluous signals and correspondence;

e) transmitting without correct identification;

f) occupation of one particular channel under poor conditions;

g) use of offensive language.

4. Repetition

Repetition of words and phrases should be avoided unless specifically requested by the receiving station.

5. Power reduction

When possible, the lowest transmitter power necessary for satisfactory communication should be used.

6. Communications with shore stations

Instructions given on communication matters by shore stations should be obeyed.

Communications should be carried out on the channel indicated by the shore station. When a change of channel is requested, this should be acknowledged by the ship.

On receiving instructions from a shore station to stop transmitting, no further communications should be made until otherwise notified (the shore station may be receiving distress or safety messages and any other transmissions could cause interference).

7. Communications with other ships

During ship-to-ship communications the ship called should indicate the channel on which further transmissions should take place. The calling ship should acknowledge acceptance before changing channel.

The listening procedure outlined above should be followed before communications are commenced on the chosen channel.

8. Distress communications

Distress calls/messages have absolute priority over all other communications. When hearing them all other transmissions should cease and a listening watch should be kept.

Any distress call/message should be recorded in the ship's log and passed to the master.

On receipt of a distress message, if in the vicinity, immediately acknowledge receipt. If not in the vicinity, allow a short interval of time to elapse before acknowledging receipt of the message in order to permit ships nearer to the distress to do so.

9. Calling

Whenever possible, a working frequency should be used. If a working frequency is not available, Channel 16 may be used, provided it is not occupied by a distress call/message.

In case of difficulty establishing contact with a ship or shore station, allow adequate time before repeating the call. Do not occupy the channel unnecessarily and try another channel.

10. Changing channels

If communications on a channel are unsatisfactory, indicate change of channel and await confirmation.

11. Spelling

If spelling becomes necessary (e.g. descriptive names, call signs, words which could be misunderstood) use the spelling table contained in the International Code of Signals and the Radio Regulations.

12. Addressing

The words 'I' and 'You' should be used prudently. Indicate to whom they refer.

Example:

"Seaship, this is Port Radar, Port Radar, do you have a pilot?"
"Port Radar, this is Seaship, I do have a pilot."

13. Watchkeeping

Ships fitted with VHF equipment should maintain a listening watch on Channel 16 and, where practicable, Channel 13 when at sea.

In certain cases governments may require ships to keep a watch on other channels.

BOOKING A COURSE OR EXAMINATION

Courses and examinations are available at any RYA Training Centre recognised for Short Range Certificate Training.

For a list of centres visit the RYA website: www.rya.org.uk/training or tel: 0845 345 0384

For serving servicemen, examinations are administered by Service Sailing Associations.

RYA Membership

Promoting and Protecting Boating
www.rya.org.uk

RYA Membership

Promoting and Protecting Boating

The RYA is the national organisation which represents the interests of everyone who goes boating for pleasure.

The greater the membership, the louder our voice when it comes to protecting members' interests.

Apply for membership today, and support the RYA, to help the RYA support you.

Benefits of Membership

- Special members' discounts on a range of products and services including boat insurance, books, charts, DVDs and class certificates
- Access to expert advice on all aspects of boating from legal wrangles to training matters
- Free issue of Certificates of Competence, increasingly asked for by everyone from overseas governments to holiday companies, insurance underwriters to boat hirers

- Access to the wide range of RYA publications, including the quarterly magazine
- Third Party insurance for windsurfing members
- Free Internet access with RYA-Online
- Special discounts on AA membership
- Regular offers in RYA Magazine
- ...and much more

Delilah

JOIN NOW

Membership form opposite or join online at *www.rya.org.uk*

Visit our website for information, advice, members' services and web shop.

1 **Important** To help us comply with Data Protection legislation, please tick *either* Box A or Box B (you must tick Box A to ensure you receive the full benefits of RYA membership). The RYA will not pass your data to third parties.

☐ **A.** I wish to join the RYA and receive future information on member services, benefits and offers by post and email.

☐ **B.** I wish to join the RYA but do not wish to receive future information on member services, benefits and offers by post and email.

When completed, please send this form to: RYA, RYA House, Ensign Way, Hamble, Southampton, SO31 4YA

2

Title	Forename	Surname	Date of Birth			Male	Female
1.			D D / M M / Y Y				
2.			D D / M M / Y Y				
3.			D D / M M / Y Y				
4.			D D / M M / Y Y				

Address

Town **County** **Post Code**

Evening Telephone **Daytime Telephone**

email

Signature: _____ Date: _____

3 **Type of membership required:** *(Tick Box)*

☐ *Personal* Annual rate £39 or £36 by Direct Debit

☐ *Under 21* Annual rate £13 (no reduction for Direct Debit)

☐ *Family** Annual rate £58 or £55 by Direct Debit

* *Family Membership: 2 adults plus any under 21's all living at the same address*

4 Please tick ONE box to show your main boating interest.

☐ Yacht Racing ☐ Yacht Cruising
☐ Dinghy Racing ☐ Dinghy Cruising
☐ Personal Watercraft ☐ Inland Waterways
☐ Powerboat Racing ☐ Windsurfing
☐ Motor Boating ☐ Sportsboats and RIBs

Please see Direct Debit form overleaf

RYA

Instructions to your Bank or Building Society to pay by Direct Debit

Please complete this form and return it to:
Royal Yachting Association, RYA House, Ensign Way, Hamble, Southampton, Hampshire SO31 4YA

DIRECT Debit

To The Manager: Bank/Building Society

Address:

Post Code:

2. Name(s) of account holder(s)

3. Branch Sort Code

		—			—		

4. Bank or Building Society account number

Banks and Building Societies may not accept Direct Debit instructions for some types of account

Cash, Cheque, Postal Order enclosed £

Made payable to the Royal Yachting Association

Office use only: Membership Number Allocated

077

Originators Identification Number

9	5	5	2	1	3

5. RYA Membership Number (For office use only)

6. Instruction to pay your Bank or Building Society

Please pay Royal Yachting Association Direct Debits from the account detailed in this instruction subject to the safeguards assured by The Direct Debit Guarantee.
I understand that this instruction may remain with the Royal Yachting Association and, if so, details will be passed electronically to my Bank/Building Society.

Signature(s)

Date

Office use / Centre Stamp